Google Classroom

Manage your classes, engage your students and learn how to use Google classroom for your lessons, assignments and grades

BY

SCOTT WEB

All trademarks and brands within this book are for clarifying purposes only and are the owned by the owners themselves, not affiliated with this document.

Table of Content

Introduction

Google Classroom is a blended school learning platform that aims to simplify the creation, distribution, and grading of assignments in a fully electronic format. It was launched following its public release on 12 August 2014 as a feature of Google Apps for Education.

Google Classroom is a feature in Google Apps that allows teachers to quickly create and arrange assignments, provide input, and interact easily with their students.

In this book, you will learn the process of creating and gathering assignments: Classroom weaves, Google Docs, Drive, and Gmail to help teachers generate and receive assignments paperless. They can easily see who completed the research or who didn't and provide direct, real-time feedback to individual students after reading this book.

How should teachers make announcements, ask questions, and comment on real-time contact with students both inside and outside of class? Is thoroughly explained in detail and steps.

How the classroom creates Drive folders automatically for each assignment, and each student is also explained in this guide.

Google Classroom ties together all of Google's offerings to help educational institutions transition to a paperless education system.

As the classroom becomes increasingly paperless, teachers need to find solutions for handing out assignments, manage their classrooms, and communicate with students. This is the complete solution for students and teachers with brief details and steps

An increasingly growing number of teachers find their way into Google Classroom. An ingenious virtual classroom with less focus on tech and more emphasis on teaching. You do not be a trained tech to navigate this classroom.

I'll explain what Google Classroom is, what you can or can't do with it in this book. You will learn to set up your classroom afterward, and I have explained several google classroom tips that you can use in conjunction with Google Classroom.

Read this book carefully to find answers to the most commonly asked teachers' questions about google classroom, plus all kinds of details on how you can use Google Classroom for your students. Students will also learn about joining a google classroom, submitting and assignments, and many more things that are only related to students. Here we go!

Chapter 1: What is Google Classroom

Google Classroom is a free application. The platform helps to connect teachers and students and can be used to coordinate and manage education. Google Classroom is considered an important paperless teaching application to help teachers and students.

The program also allows teachers to teach from a distance, which can provide much-needed help in the current situation.

1.1 Google Classroom and its Working Principle

It's hard to avoid the most popular tools Google has to offer — Gmail, Google Calendar, and Google Docs are now staples to get organized and work done. Such collaboration tools have revolutionized the way in which we interact, collaborate, and store information online. The educationally-friendly Google Classroom platform brings the benefits of paperless networking and interactive communication to classrooms for teachers and students. Tens of millions of teachers and students in thousands of schools around the world use Google Classroom, making it one of the most common Edtech resources today.

Google describes Google Classroom as "Your classroom mission control," and this may be the easiest way to think about it. It is a platform for teachers and students to link Google's G Suite tools together. From there, you can choose which features you wish to incorporate. This flexibility, and its seamless integration with the popular Google tools, is probably what has made Google Classroom one of today's most widely used edtech tools.

Is Google Classroom an LMS?

Google Classroom is not a stand-alone system for learning management (LMS), course management (CMS), or student information (SIS) system. Google adds new functions to Google Classroom periodically. For example, in June 2019, Google revealed that schools would soon be in a position to synchronize the latest grading features of the app with an existing student information system. As Google continues to add features, it is likely to start looking, and more like an LMS. But it's best, for now, to think of the tool as a one-stop-shop for class organizing.

In most cases, teachers and students can use a Google account provided by their school to access Google Classroom. While the primary users of Google Classroom are teachers and students in schools, there are also features that administrators, families, and homeschoolers can use.

1.2 Features & Benefits of Google Classroom

As the classroom becomes increasingly paperless, teachers need to start finding solutions for handing out assignments, managing their classroom, and communicating with students.

An increasingly growing number of teachers find their way into Google Classroom. An ingenious immersive classroom with less emphasis on software and more emphasis on teaching. You do not be a professional tech to handle this classroom.

I'll explain in this post what is Google Classroom, and what you can or can't do with it. You will learn to set up your classroom afterward, and I'll give you some great apps that you can use in combination with Google Classroom.

What is Google Classroom?

Google Classroom is a free software program developed by Google. Google Classroom helps teachers and students connect and can be used to coordinate and handle tasks, go paperless, collaborate with students and teachers, teach from afar, and so on! You could compare it to Showbie, as well as other online learning platforms or management systems.

It is built on top of Google Docs and Google Drive, which means that any teacher can use it very easily and intuitively. But that doesn't mean that it's boring. Google Classroom is packed with surprises that you will find along the way. I hope this post will get you started with the fundamentals.

Things you can do with Google Classroom

So that's probably the biggest question. How should you use the Classroom on Google? What's for you in it?

It's completely fair, first of all. You 're not going to need to upgrade to a premium edition, which will save you more money. Yeah, $0.00. None of that. At. At. That. That.

You can get started after you have configured your classroom. In just a few minutes, you'll find out how to set up your Google Classroom account. Let me first show you why Google Classroom's a big deal. Here's a rundown of what you should do about it:

Add announcements and lesson material: Give advertisements about your lesson to your students. In the announcements, add the lesson materials. Such announcements will appear in the Google Classroom stream of your students. That way, the students can quickly find everything. We can add materials from a Google drive, connect to that lesson in Google Classroom, add files and pictures from your computer, add a YouTube video, or add any other link that your students want to see. That is so easy!

Add assignments: You may add an assignment to your course just as you add an announcement. It works the same way, but you get the option of adding a due date and grading it here. If they have to make an assignment, it will alert the students, and it will also appear in their calendar. You can also add an assignment to the Book Widgets in just a few minutes.

Degree an assignment: You can then check and grade the assignments your students have given in. There's room for feedback via a comment from a teacher. Then, return the task to your students. The "Points" tab houses a grade book of the assignments and grades of all the students.

Manage students: Your students must, of course, be able to share their comments. Or don't they? That is entirely up to you! You can manage permissions, allow students to post and comment, comment only, or give the teacher the ability to post and comment only. Even your students can be emailed individually.

Things you can't do with Google Classroom

It's an online learning platform, but it's not a chatbox: you can comment on assignments and announcements, but no chat function is available. You can send them an email if you want to be in direct contact with your students, or you can allow other Google apps to take over this function. Think about Meet Hangouts.

A test or a quiz tool: When it comes to making quizzes in Google Classroom, there are several possibilities, but it's still not supposed to be a quiz tool. To that end, there are so many other good features. Think of the quizzes regarding Google Forms or Book Widgets.

Option 1: Just inside Google Classroom, you can add tests and assignments from other educational apps, such as a Book Widgets test that is automatically graded.

Option 2: Inside Google Classroom itself, here's what you can do: add a question. Then choose between an open answer and a question with multiple choices. I admit, not that impressive. If you want your digital classroom to become more interactive, the best option is to choose the first.

How do teachers use Google Classroom?

Because it is a fairly flexible platform, educators take advantage of its features in many different ways. Teachers can use Google Classroom to:

Simplify how they treat schools. The app integrates with other sites such as Google Docs, Drive, and Calendar, and there are plenty of built-in "shortcuts" to handle classroom tasks.

Organize, distribute, and collect assignments, materials for the course, and student work digitally. Teachers may also post an assignment to different classes, or year after year adjust and repeat assignments. Google Classroom can help you avoid some photocopier trips and reduce some of the shuffling of paper that comes with teaching and learning if your students have regular access to the devices.

Ask the students about the classwork: You can use the site to post updates and comments about assignments, and it's easy to see who finished or didn't finish their work. You can also privately check in with individual students, answer their questions, and offer support.

Give timely feedback to the students on their assignments and evaluations. Google Forms can be used inside Google Classroom to build and exchange quizzes, which are automatically graded as students turn them in. Not only do you spend less time grading, but your students will provide instant feedback on their work.

Do teachers use Google Classroom to teach live, like with Zoom?

Google provides Hangouts Meet's premium features free to teachers and students who are at home during the coronavirus pandemic, allowing for virtual meetings with up to 250 people as well as live streaming. The recording feature in Hangouts Meet, in addition, to live video capabilities, gives teachers an easy tool to create pre-recorded lesson videos for students to watch at their own time.

How do I set up my Google Classroom?

Google Classroom 's basic setup process is fairly intuitive, even for first-time users. The Google Teacher Center offers several tutorials to get started — if you are looking for the most up-to-date videos and information, this is your best bet. There are also plenty of do-it-yourself tutorials posted by professors and tech integration specialists on YouTube. Many of these videos created by teachers include practical tips and tricks they have learned in their own classrooms from using the platform.

What is Google doing with my students' data? Should I be worried about privacy?

As an educator, protecting the privacy and data of your students should definitely be a consideration when choosing a digital tool for your classroom. Whenever a tool may collect student data, it's important to ask questions about how the companies involved secure, use, or store student data. For more information, please read our complete Google Classroom Privacy Review.

Google says privacy and protection of data is a top priority for all G Suite for Education products.

However, educators should bear in mind that there is a right for parents and families to opt-out if they don't want their children using Google products in school.

Until Google Classroom is released, school administrators and teachers may wish to have an alternate plan in place for students who may opt-out.

What's more, Google's prominence in branding and school products has raised questions about the trade-offs that allow Google to build its brand in schools. Whether you're using Google Classroom or not, it's important to get students to think critically about data privacy and the marketing we see in various aspects of our lives-including our classrooms.

How can Google Classroom support differentiation in the classroom?

Google Classroom may help streamline the formative assessment, which is essential to benefit students who may need more support or additional challenges. Google Classroom may, in a way, make it easier and faster to gather regular feedback on the progress of your students. There are, of course, plenty of other formative assessment tools out there, many of which now offer Google Classroom integrations.

Google Classroom also makes it easier for individual students or small groups to customize assignments. This means teachers may give other students or groups in a class changed or different assignments. The ability to do all of this online may make the distinction efforts of teachers less visible for the class, something that could be beneficial to students who might feel singled out.

Differentiation will always be a matter of creative problem-solving with or without a tool like Google Classroom, and there is no one or "right" way to do that. Fortunately, many teachers share online their tips, tricks, and creative solutions. Here is an example of how Google Classroom is used by one teacher to meet students at their level.

What's new in Google Classroom?

Since its launch, the platform has been updated quite a bit, and Google continues to regularly introduce new features, often based on teacher feedback. For many years, users lament the lack of grading features or a tool for building rubrics in Google Classroom. Google has listened to and is deploying a new tool for collecting and grading work, called Assignments, late in the school year 2019-2020.

Consider switching up the types of tools you share with them in Google Classroom to make learning with digital content more interactive for students. Aside from G Suite tools such as Google Docs and Google Slides, teachers and students can share other media types, including images, website links, YouTube videos, and screencasts. Some teachers even provide a variety of options for students to submit their work within Google Classroom. For example, you might give students the option to reply with a comment, video clip, or drawing to a reading assignment that demonstrates their thought.

If you are looking to create an interactive hub for students, you may be considering doing so on the Stream page of Google Classroom. The stream is a feed within Google Classroom where everybody in the class can find announcements and upcoming assignments, and it is the first thing students see when they log in. Alice Keeler, a well-known writer who writes extensively about Google Classroom, advises that you use the stream to post your class agenda and suggest that you use Screencastify to post student video messages.

Some teachers set up class discussion boards using the Web, where students can interact online by asking questions or commenting on the posts. Such discussion boards will help improve class engagement and give students greater fairness in getting teachers to hear (or read) their voices.

You could use the stream as a closed social chat network of sorts, and it can be a great way to help children learn in a "walled garden" style setting, using all sorts of different interactive communication skills.

Hidden Features of Google Classroom

In the last two years, Google Classroom has grown into a popular learning platform. With the ability to integrate G Suite tools such as Google Docs, Google Slides, Google Sheets, Gmail, and Google Calendar seamlessly, Google Classroom creates an efficient workflow for teachers and students through an easy-to-navigate online environment that organizes assignments and content in class.

Although Google Classroom offers many great affordances, three, in particular, can save a lot of time for teachers and students, and also improve the productivity of workflow. So, let's exploit those exciting features!

The Assignment Calendar

To help keep students and teachers focused, Google Classroom automatically produces an Assignment Calendar. Each time a teacher generates an assignment or query inside Google Classroom and adds a due date to it, the assignment immediately appears within Google Classroom on the class calendar.

Select the three lines in the top-left corner of the screen to find this calendar, and then select Calendar. Teachers and students can view work that has been assigned to the class with this screen displayed.

Teachers will also notice that their G Suite Calendar now features a new Calendar. Not only can teachers add assignments through the Classroom to this calendar, but they can also access it directly through the G Suite Calendar to add activities that may not be tied to a due date for the class.

Some examples of teachers who use this calendar feature include: arranging field trips for students, setting up extra tutoring time and planning an after-school meeting. Consider making the calendar more accessible in the Calendar settings, and then sharing the URL link with parents.

The Work Area

The work area inside Google Classroom can also be used by teachers and students to collect all outstanding assignments in one location. If a teacher has not graded a given assignment, it will show up in this field. Similarly, if a student has not turned into an assignment, it will also show up in their area of work. The work area can, therefore, serve as a default task list and help teachers and students to effectively identify and manage their workflow.

Organize the class stream with Topics

Topics, a new feature inside Google Classroom, allows teachers to organize the posts they add to the "Stream" classroom. Teachers can now assign a topic when creating an announcement, assignment, or question, and these topics act as a category for each post, enabling them to be organized effectively.

Whenever a new topic is created, it will show all posts on the left side of the Classroom Stream that has been assigned to that topic and will appear if a topic is selected. The feature Topics now allows teachers to coordinate all material within their course. For example, a history teacher may create a topic for each study unit, such as "Ancient Rome." For each unit or chapter, they study, a math teacher might choose to create a topic.

Share to Classroom Extension

The Chrome Extension Share to Classroom allows teachers to easily display and share student work and screens with the class for teachers who use Chromebooks or laptops in their classrooms. Students can share a web site with their teacher's computer using the Share to Classroom extension. Students click on the extension first, then pick Move to Instructor. Once done, the teacher receives a pop-up notification on her screen that she will have to accept before displaying the student's page.

The extension also lets teachers build material from Google Classroom right from the extension. If a teacher finds a website that he would like to post as part of an assignment, question, or announcement in Google Classroom, using the extension, he can create any of those options.

By making use of the Share to Classroom extension, teachers and students can now quickly and efficiently share new insights and stories.

1.3 How to Create Edit and Delete Google Classroom

How to build a Google class with Classroom?

- Surf through https:/classroom.google.com
- Click the "+" sign next to your Google Account in the top right corner
- Select "Create Class" and give it a name and section, then click "Build."

For your class, the "Section" field is a secondary descriptor, so you may want to add anything like 1st period, a grade point, or some other short definition. To build your first class, click the Plus sign.

Customize the Appearance of Your Class

You'll be given a default header image when you first create your class. This is the image students will see when they click on the assignments and announcements to access your class. With a few quick steps, you can customize that image.

- You will find "Change Class Theme" in the bottom right corner of the image
- Click on the "Change Class Theme" button to open a photo gallery to choose from for your class.
- Choose the photo from the gallery, then click on "Choose Class Theme" to change the image in your header.

There are a number of pictures to choose from, but most are on some sort of academic subject matter. For example, you could select books for classes in Language Arts, a piano for music, colored pencils for art, and so on. Check out the picture gallery you can use to personalize your class.

Adding Students to Your Classes

Once all the classes you need have been developed, you can easily add students to your roster. These can be done by following the instructions below.

- Click on the class you would like to register for
- Note the class code (on the left) and distribute it to the students.
- Students can then navigate to https:/classroom.google.com, click on the "+" sign in the top right corner of the page, and pick "Join."
- Students enter the class code and are added to the class immediately.

Note that teacher can change or deactivate the class code at any time. Just click the drop-down next to the code for the class and choose to reset or disable it as you feel the need.

Resetting or disabling the code won't impact students who have already enrolled in your class.

The class code can be reset or deactivated via the drop-down menu at any time.

Edit or Delete a Class

When you try out Google Classroom for the first time, you might end up creating some test classes just to get a feel for everything it has to offer. This is perfectly normal because we all want to try out new products and see if they're going to work for us. However, if you're done, you may want to edit your test class name or simply delete it altogether. Here's how to get it done.

- In the top left corner of the screen, click the menu button (looks like three horizontal lines)
- Just click the 3 dots at the top right corner of the class you would like to edit
- Use Rename or Delete to make the required changes

1.4 Setting up Google Classroom

Google Classroom set up in easy measures

Okay, I've got you up until now. That means something Google Classroom needs to mean to you. You should find it easy to set up and very intuitive to continue to use it. Follow those steps to set up your teacher account at Google Classroom:

Sign up

We can use the Classroom by logging in using a G suite email address when you go to classroom.google.com, or you can use it for educational purposes without having to use a "letter." That way, everything works just fine too. If you have hundreds of them, it's only harder to handle your pupils. You 're going to have to add that one by one.

Create your first class

In the upper right corner, click on the "+" tab. Select "Create a Class" You fill in some info about your class here. Write down a name and section of a good class. The name of the class should be your class title so that you can find it back in a few seconds. Then click the Create button.

Invite students to your class

You can then invite your students once you have created your class. Let them sign by entering the unique code you've given them using the Google Classroom app. You can find the code in your class which was developed. Go to the "students'" tab. Another choice is to allow your students to enter their email address, one by one. One thing you should keep in mind: your students need an email address from Gmail or Google.

You can also visit classroom.google.com to let your students go. You can select "join class" there, enter the class code, and you are in! This might be a little easier because you don't have to type in the email address of every student.

Now ready for your online class! At least, it's there, and it's accessible to everyone. You have to do a few other things before you can take off for real.

Make the first work or advertise

We can share a first announcement in the Path, or go to Classwork-click the "+ Build" button and share your first Google Classroom assignment. Don't forget to have your assignments numbered. Your students will find it easier to see which one comes first as you can't reorder assignments in the stream. You can, however, move assignments up to the top. Click on the title to see if there are any students in the assignment, and to give grades and feedback. You can then return the assignments to your students so that they can start editing again.

Add some lesson material to your class/assignment

Fill in Google Drive material or add a YouTube video, a computer file, a connection, etc. You will find those options right below the due date. If you just want to share your class presentation, which is not linked to an assignment, you can go to the "About" tab. A few lesson materials like slides, interesting articles, and examples can be added here.

Log in to the Drive folder

Each time you create a new class, Google Classroom creates a Drive folder for that class. In your class, you can access the folder by going to all tiles. One folder icon can be found on each piece of tile. Click on it in the folder you are. You can add materials for the class here too. All the assignments of your students will eventually end up in the Google Drive tab, so you can find it back whenever you wish.

Chapter 2: Google Classroom for Teachers

An increasingly growing number of teachers find their way into Google Classroom. An ingenious immersive classroom with less emphasis on software and more emphasis on teaching. You do not be a professional tech to handle this classroom.

2.1 Google Classroom- Sign-up for Teachers

How can teacher sign-up for Google Classroom?

In order to use Google Classroom in a school with students, a free G Suite for Education account must be signed in to your school. If your school already has an account, then you@yourschool.edu could look like this.

But if you are an educator who is conducting courses outside of school, you can also sign up with your personal account (you@example.com). In such cases, a G Suite for Education account is not compulsory.

You can subscribe to Google Classroom anyway by visiting **classroom.google.com.**

How does Google Classroom relate to G Suite for Education?

Google Classroom is a framework for learning management that is part of the G Suite for Education platform. It is fully integrated with other applications in the G Suite such as Docs, Slides, Drive, etc.

What are the criteria or guidelines for using Google Classroom?

Some of the major accentuations:

- Google Classroom requires an active internet connection to work

- All data is saved on your Google Drive without the need for local servers
- Google Classroom applications can be found on both Android and iOS apps

How to set up your Google Classroom?

Google Classroom can be set up fairly easily. Here are the relevant steps:

- Build a class by clicking on the '+' button on the home screen at the top right. You will need to add the name of the class, the subject name, and the section in question.
- To customize the course description, click the 'About' tab, or add course materials such as links and syllabi.
- To invite your students to enter the classroom, click on the 'Students' tab either submit invitations or give them a 'Learning code.'
- Choose the student attendance level from the 'Students' tab.
- Visit the 'About' tab to add the co-teachers.
- You can then select a Classroom theme and upload a cover photo as well.
- Review your preferences for notification by logging in to Settings. You can do so by clicking the extreme left on the Tribar button.
- Click the '+' icon to access the core features of the platform: Reuse Post, Create Question, create assignment, and Create Ads.

2.2 Accepting Administrative Rights of a Classroom

The administrator who manages the Classroom will be able to build classes for you and add students. If they invite you to their classroom to be a co-teacher, you'll need to accept the invitation.

To approve or reject the lessons, you must sign in to the Classroom before they are available to any student or co-teacher.

- Go to the.google.com.
- Click Accept on Class card.
- Confirm student number and class activation, and press Approve.

Change Your Profile Photo

- Click the Menu at the top left-hand side
- Scroll down and press Customize.
- Click Change under the Profile photo.
- Click on a photo or drag it from your computer.
- (Optional)The box above your picture is resized.
- Click Set as photo profile.

Customize your Notifications

- Click Menu at the top left.
- Click Settings in the bottom left-hand corner (you may need to scroll down).
- Click any notice to switch it on or off.
- (Optional)Click Shutdown to turn off all alerts while receiving email notifications

Change the class theme

You can change the default image or color pattern that is displayed at the top of the class stream after you create a class. Only a teacher can change the subject matter.

Select another theme pictures from the gallery

- Click the class you are administering and click the button on the right-hand side of the page in small letters.

The option of choice

- Choose an image from the gallery and then click Choose the theme of the class.

- Choose Shapes, select color, and pattern, and then Choose a Class style.

Upload image to your own theme

- You can also upload a custom cover photo similar to a Facebook photo for your class.

Open the file, and click the picture at the bottom.

The option of choice

- Drag a picture into the center of the screen from your phone.
- Just Click Select a photo from your computer and select the image you want your class to use and click Open.
- Click the Class theme selected.

Change Class Name and Description

- Make sure you 're in the "Google Classroom" main page to change your class name and description by clicking on the upper left corner of the screen.
- Click on the drop-down menu.
- Click the button in the corner on the class description box you wish to change.
- From there, you can edit your class name, line, and topic.

Adding a topic

- Go to the left side of the Stream page to add a topic, and click the button
- Type the topic name in the word prompt
- Click the Add to topic button

The tab (+)

Making an Announcement

- Click the class below
- Click + and then click Create post at the bottom right corner of the page.

- Enter your message in the Share box with your class.
- Click POST to post an announcement

Attach a File from Your Computer

- Press the Clip icon on paper
- Click Select your computer files, find the file on your computer, and then double-click the file.
- Click Download

Attach a File from Google Drive

- Click the icon on the Google Drive
- Choose file, then click Add file

Attach a YouTube Video

- Click the YouTube icon here
- Use the search bar to search for a video. When the video has been found click Add

Attach a Link

- Click on the icon for a link
- Paste a link in the box Link
- Click LINK-ADD

2.3 Creating an Assignment in Google Classroom

How to set up a Google Classroom Assignment

Create a Task

- Log in.
- Click here.
- Swing over Add in the bottom click Create assignment.
- Enter the title and indicate some directions.

Change due date or time of assignment

The assignment is due by default the next day. Changing it to:

- Press the arrow Down next to Due Tomorrow.

- Select the date and then pick the date.
- (Optional) Click time and type a time to set a due time.
- Click on the due date to create an assignment, and click Remove next to the date.

Add materials to an assignment

You may add attachments to your assignments, such as Google Drive files, YouTube videos, or links.

- Click Attach to upload a file, select a file and then click Upload.

To add a Drive object, for example, a document or a form

- Drive. Click.
- Select the object and click Add.

Just click the Down arrow button next to the attachment to determine how the students communicate with the attachment and choose the option:

- Students can view the file — the file can be read by the students, but not changed.
- Students can edit files — Students can make file changes.
- Make a copy for each student — The students receive a copy of the file that they can change.

To attach a YouTube video

- Press Check for a Picture.
- Indicate keywords in the search bar.
- Click the Video button and then press Connect.

To attach a video link

- Press URL icon.
- Type the URL in and click Add.
- Click Link to connect a page, enter the URL and then press Add.
- Click Mouse next to the attachment to uninstall attachment.

Post a multiple class assignment

- (Optional) Press the Down arrow at the bottom, next to the class name.
- Check the appropriate box next to the class you want to include.

How to create a Google Classroom Assignment on Android

- Tap The class Classroom.
- Tap Assignment to Add.
- Enter the title and indicate some directions.

Change due date or time of assignment

The task is due the next day by default, but you can change it.

- Tap Due date, pick another date and tap end.
- (Optional) Tap Time, select time, then tap finish.
- Add in the assignment materials

Your assignment may include Drive files, links, images, or YouTube videos

- Tap Attach and select the file, and tap Upload to upload the file
- Tap Drive, tap Element, and tap Select to attach a Drive item.
- To determine how students, communicate with an attachment, tap the attachment next to it

Examine and select an option

- Students may edit files — Students may make file changes.
- Students may view the file — students may read the file, but they may not change it.
- Make a copy for each student — Students receive a copy of the file they can change.

Delete — Remove the attachment

- Tap Connect, enter URL, and tap Add to add a connection.

- Tap up Upload to add a file.
- Tap Camera to add a photo, take or pick a photo, and click OK.
- Tap YouTube to add a YouTube video, and select an option:

To search for a video to attach

- Tap Search for a Video.
- Indicate keywords in the search bar.
- Tap Video, then tap Add.

To attach a video link

- Click on URL.
- Insert the URL, and press Add.
- Tap Preview next to the attachment name to uninstall a file, and select Uninstall.

Post a multiple class assignment

- Tap Add next to the class name.
- Select any further classes that have been done.

How to create an iOS / iPad / iPhone assignment on Google Classroom?

- Tap The class Classroom.
- Tap Assignment to Add.
- Enter the title and indicate some directions.

Change due date or time of assignment

The task is due the next day by default, but you can change it.

- Tap Due date, select another date and tap OK.
- (Optional) Tap Add time, choose the time, and press OK.
- (Optional) To create an assignment that has no due date, tap Remove at Due tomorrow.

Add materials to an assignment

To your assignment, you can add Drive files, links, pictures, or photos.

- Tap Add.
- Tap Drive, and tap the item to attach the Drive item.

Tap Preview and choose the option: To decide how students interact with an attachment next to the attachment.

- Students may edit files — Students may make file changes.
- Students may view the file — students may read the file, but they may not change it.
- Make a copy for each student — Students receive a copy of the file they can change.

Delete — Remove the attachment

- Tap Connect, enter URL, and tap Add to add a connection.
- Tap Choose a photo and choose your photo to attach a photo. Or, tap Camera Using and take a picture.
- To delete an attachment, tap Remove next to the attachment

Create an Assignment in Google Classroom (Part 1 Details)

Within Google, Classroom assignments can be created and assigned to students, and there are a variety of useful choices for educators here. Here is how to add your first allocation.

- Select the class you would like to submit an assignment to
- Now click "Attribution" at the center of the page
- Give a title to your assignment and add any further instructions or descriptions in the box below
- Click the date to select your assignment due date and add time if you want to specify when the assignment is due on a given day
- Choose the assignment type that you wish to create by clicking on one of the icons next to the Assign word. Your choices include uploading a file from your computer,

inserting a Google Drive file, adding a YouTube video, or adding a link to a website.

- Click the "Assign" button to give your students the assignment.

If we want to give the assignment to more than one class, click on the class name at the bottom of the assignment window and select the classes to which you wish to assign it.

Create a Google Classroom Assignment (Part 2 Details)

Many teachers using Google Classroom are likely to choose to add an assignment from their Drive, as this is probably where many of the teacher's resources are now stored. However, selecting a Drive tool in Google Classroom has an added advantage, and this becomes obvious with the choices you get when selecting a file from the Drive.

- Students can view the file: If you want all students to be able to view the file, select this option, but not be able to modify it.
- Students can edit files: If you want all students to be able to edit and work on the same paper, choose this. This would be best for a collaborative class project where students in the same Google Presentation may work on separate slides, or where they are collaboratively brainstorming ideas for something you want to discuss in your next class.
- Make a copy for each student: If you choose this option, the Classroom will make a copy of the original file for each student in your classroom and give them the editing rights to the file. The master of the instructor shall remain intact, and the students shall have no access to the original register. Choose this is you want a paper that has an essay question for students to work on quickly, or a digital worksheet template where students fill in the blanks with their own responses.

This level of automation was possible before Google Classroom, but when integrated into this new platform, it is infinitely easier to manage.

Teachers have a range of choices on how they want to exchange Drive assignments.

2.4 Edit Announcements, Assignments, and Quizzes

- Click on the button at the top right of the announcement to edit an announcement that has already been posted on your class account.
- Press Change icon.
- You can edit the content words of the post, or if your post is an assignment, you can edit the Due Date and which topic it is also posted in.
- Once the post has been edited, click the button, and it will update your post. The students in your classroom should receive a notice that the post is being changed.

Edit announcement that is scheduled or drafted

If you saved a post in your classroom but have not yet posted it, you can still edit the message.

- If you saved a post to use later on in the middle of your stream page, click on the option.
- Tap on your Drafts post to edit what you've got up to now.
- Once your draft has been completely edited, click on the button.
- If your draft is scheduled, press the button after you have edited your draft instead of clicking on the Post button.

Edit already posted quizzes

If you have posted and assigned this already, you can delete it.

- Click on the button at the top of the page to get to your assignment.
- Click the button on the left-hand side of the page.
- Click on which assignment you want to delete.
- You can edit the assignment once there, as you wish. The edits should auto-save.

If you edit an assignment, your classroom students won't receive a notification of that. Be sure to post an announcement in your class to inform the students that you have made changes to an assignment.

Add Students to your Classroom

Add students by an invitation email.

- Click on the button at the top of the page center.
- Press the upper-page button.
- Click where it says to
- Enter the student's email you wish to invite. If you've previously emailed them, you can simply insert their name in the file, and their email will show up below where you typed. You can at once invite over one student.
- Once all the students you would like to invite have entered, click on the button. They'll receive an email inviting them to become a student in your class.

Add students via class code

- The class code will appear on the page of your class on the left.
- Use this code to ask students to join your class, which is different for each class.

Adding Teachers

- Click here for a lesson.
- Scroll over at the end.
- Then click the button

- Insert the teacher's email address you wish to invite into the text prompt provided
- After adding all the teachers, click the button next to a particular teacher's name to show other choices
- Click Remove Teacher from Class
- To make the teacher the highest level administrator of the class, click Make class owner. The only person who can take other teachers out of the class is the class owner

Restricting Access to Files

- Click here for a lesson.
- Scroll over at the end.

Click the Class Drive Folder button

- Only the Administrators can view the Class Drive Folder
- When students open the Class Drive Folder, they will only see files shared with them (i.e., files placed in the class by the announcement, assignment, or question);
- Right-click a class-shared file and then press Sharing button
- Page that pops up below:
- Click the Update button
- Page that should pop up as follows:

If there is an alias for a student, then the file selected is a shared file. The file otherwise was NOT shared.

- Click Change button and click Off-Specific Individuals
- Click the student alias down arrow on the right and click the View Only button
- Check the options Disable download, print and copy option for commenters and viewers
- Click Save then Finished button when the sharing settings are changed

2.5 Grading and Returning Assignments to Students

Grading Assignments

- Grade a Form Assignment
- Click on a class
- Click on the Done / Not Done option

The following page should pop-up. This is the Grading page:

To access the student responses, click on the Assignment Name. A new tab should open with the form Click on the student answers button Click on the Responses tab (next to the Question Stab). The next page should be:

- Each student's response can be corrected manually by the administrator
- Once a mark (i.e., grade) sheet has been developed, each student's marks can be inputted beside
- Their name by navigating to the Grading page
- Press the Return button to finalize the marks given to the student. Once the Return button has been clicked, the students will be informed that their assignment has been graded

Grade a File Upload Assignment

- Navigate to the Grading page
- The file upload will be given as an attachment under the student's name. Click on the name of the file to view the file upload
- Once a mark (i.e., grade) sheet has been developed, each student's marks can be inputted beside their name by navigating to the Grading page
- Press the Return button to finalize the marks given to the student. Once the Return button has been clicked, the

students will be informed that their assignment has been graded

Grading Assignments

Grade a Form Assignment

- Click on a class
- Click on the Done / Not Done option
- The following page should pop-up. This is the Grading page.
- To view the student responses, click on the Assignment Name. One new tab will open with the form Click on the student answers button Click on the Answers tab (next to the Question Stab). The following page should appear:
- Each student's response can be corrected manually by the administrator
- Once a mark (i.e., grade) sheet has been developed, each student's marks can be inputted beside

Press the Return button to finalize the marks given to the student. Once the Return button has been clicked, the students will be informed that their assignment has been graded

Grade a File Upload Assignment

- Navigate to the Grading page
- The file upload will be given as an attachment under the student's name. Click on the name of the file to view the file upload.
- Once a mark (i.e., grade) sheet has been developed, each student's marks can be inputted beside their name by navigating to the Grading page
- Press the Return button to finalize the marks given to the student. Once the Return button has been clicked, the students will be informed that their assignment has been graded.

Student marking and returning assignments

Teachers can find a number of different ways to apply for students. Perhaps the most efficient way, however, is to enter the class that you are interested in grading and clicking from the Stream view on the assigned name. Look at the sidebar at the top left of the Stream view, and you will see the "Coming Assignments" box if you notice that assignments get lost between student conversations. Click on the assignment to be evaluated, and obey the instructions below:

- Click on the name of the student who submitted an assignment you would like to grade.
- Use the commenting features in Drive to leave comprehensive feedback on specific parts of the student submission when the document opens. When you're done, close down the document. All modifications are automatically saved.
- When you return to the Classroom, click on the right-hand side of the student's name where "No grade" is stated and enter the assignment grade based points.
- Check the box next to the student you have just graded, then click the "Return" button to save the grade and notify the student that they have graded their paper.
- Add some input in the pop-up box and then press "Return Assignment."

Grades entered by the teacher will automatically trigger a student's email notification.

Grading Tips and Further Information

How do the students think I was grading their assignment? Am I required to grade an assignment out of 100? These questions are answered, and more, below.

- When a teacher returns a student's assignment, the teacher no longer has the rights to edit that document.

- You can return a student's assignment without grading it by simply checking the box next to the name of the student and clicking Return. That may be useful for error-submitted assignments.
- When you return a student's assignment they will automatically receive an email notification informing them of your actions
- At any time, you can change the grade by clicking on the grade and then clicking "Update."
- The Google Drive folder where all student submissions are stored is opened by clicking the folder button. This is useful for a one-time review of all the assignments submitted.
- The default number of points for an assignment is 100, but this can be changed by clicking on the drop-down arrow and choosing another value, entering a different value manually, or even the option not to score.

2.6 Google Classroom- Advance User Tips for Teachers

Google Classroom Teacher Tips

Google Classroom is among K-12's most popular digital tools.

Over the years, it has greatly improved, and teachers have learned how to make the most of this flexible assignment manager and communication hub.

The Community's shared tips are AWESOME!

These are FOR teachers, and recommended by teachers!

Use Control + F to Find Numbers and Words in Classroom

After a few weeks of assignments, even the most structured Classwork page can get very long.

To search for keywords or assignment numbers (as mentioned above) on the page, use the keyboard shortcut, Control + F (Command+F on a mac). Teach that trick to students, too!

Choose the Topics Organizational Strategy

Using the topics feature on the classroom page helps organize student and teacher assignments. There are many different ways to organize yourself. There are several ways this can be done, and what works for one teacher doesn't work for everyone. To teachers, this is a personal choice. Pick a technique that works for your area and grade level of content. Check out this post on How to Organize Assignments at Google Classroom for ideas.

Create a "Resources" Topic and Keep at the Top of the Classwork Page

Every class requires a place to store resources, connections, rules of class, syllabus, and so on. Mindy Barron suggests that you create a special resource and class material topic, and keep it close to the top for easy access. Make sure these files are clearly named, so students know exactly what's in there.

Create a Google Classroom Class Template

If you have selected your preferred form of organizing for Google Classroom (and checked it!), make a copy of the class as your guide. You can keep creating a copy anytime you need a new class and have all of your topics already produced and arranged, and your assignments will be saved as drafts!

To make a copy of a Google Classroom class: go to your Google Classroom home, then click on the class card's three dots and choose "copy class."

Use Direct Links to Assignments

Knew you could get a direct connection to a specific assignment? This makes referring students back to a given activity so easy.

Just go to the Classwork page, locate the assignment, right-click on the three dots, and copy the link.

Use a Google Doc as a Syllabus (Secondary)

Many teachers use Google Docs to create a syllabus so that it can be updated throughout the year as a living document. Add connections to external services, regular allocations, essential dates, etc. You can also place links to Google Classroom assignments to prevent students from being checked too long.

Break projects with separate due dates into smaller assignments

Project-based learning is so important, and as we try to move beyond the stagnant, one-and-done tasks, we need to think differently about how we execute this in our classrooms.

For students, big projects can be overwhelming, especially those who haven't learned how to manage their time. Giving them milestones and splitting the project into smaller assignments with checkpoints is critical. In fact, that's one of my book's implementation tips.

Build a Separate Enrichment and Extension Class

In my class, early completion of your assignment didn't mean either free time or games. It has included reading and learning programs for my pupils. Consider having a separate class for extension or enrichment programs within Google Classroom.

You could even gamify that idea and give digital badges to accomplish a challenge or task.

Use Private Comments for Feedback and Student Conversations

One of my Google Classroom favorite features is the private comment app. This little tool will help streamline communication and boost the feedback loop with your students.

Teacher feedback is one of the biggest factors for student development!

Private comments between you and your student are just that – private. (No-one else could read it.)

Please remember to use private comments not only at the end of the assignment but all through!

And this doesn't negate the power of face-to-face conversations, but it does help document so that students can remember the feedback, as well as give students an opportunity to communicate who don't usually speak in front of the class.

There are a couple of different places where students can add private comments.

To add a private comment from the Student Work page

- Click on the assignment for which you wish to give feedback from the Classwork tab.
- Press the "View Task" button.
- Pick Student from the left roster.
- You will see "Add Private Comment" at the bottom of the right-hand panel.
- Click to type and then add your student's private message.

You can now also add private comments from inside the student's document using the latest grading feature in Google Classroom.

Use the Grading Tool to add a private comment:

- Click on the assignment for which you wish to give feedback from the Classwork tab.
- Click the "View Assignment" button.
- Click on the student file you want to give feedback about.
- Post a private comment with the right-hand panel.

Use Private Comments for Reflection

Some teachers take private commentary features a step further and make it part of the assignment by requiring students to include a reflection as a private statement after submitting their assignment. Sean Fahey recommends using an open-ended question or gives students a prompt such as, "What did you like most about the assignment?" or "What aspect has surprised you the most?" Be sure to add this to the instructions, so they don't forget!

Attach a Template Document for Each Assignment

This tip comes to us from Michelle Baragar. She attaches a blank Google Doc or a template to each assignment as a copy for each student. In Google Classroom, you can view the assignment page and see a thumbnail for each student. This allows you to see progress, or lack thereof, at a glance.

Even if you do not have a template for your assignment, Michelle Baragar suggests attaching a saved black document to use as a template so that you can still get the thumbnail view!

Not every teacher is on board with Google Classroom. If you work with a teacher who is hesitant or maybe a little technophobic, invite them to join your class as a student or a co-teacher.

I suggest inviting them as a student at first, so they get an idea of how it works before giving them the ability to add and edit your class as a co-teacher. Co-teachers can do everything you can do in a class.

To invite teachers

- Go to the class where you want to add them,
- Then click on the People tab at the top of the page.
- To invite as a co-teacher, click on the invite teacher's icon and type their name or email address and click Invite.

- To invite a teacher as a student, click on the invite student's icon and type their name or email address and click Invite.
- 1 Create a demo student account to demonstrate Google Classroom to your students.

Google Classroom doesn't currently offer teachers a way to view their classes as a student. (I wish it did!)

So to see your class as a student, you must have a student's account. A workaround, suggested by Julie Sweeney Newton, is to use a demo account and log in as a student so you can see how the student side works and to demonstrate how to use the classroom for your students.

If you have access to create Google accounts in your school's domain, this is easy. Most teachers do not have this kind of access.

In that case, reach out to your tech coach or tech support to see if it's possible to get a demo account.

Package your Digital Assignments

This tip is a collection of tips to improve how your instructions and package everything students will need into your Google Classroom assignments.

These tips come from a previous post and infographic, how to Package Your Digital Assignments.

Chapter 3: Google Classroom for Students

Google classroom has numerous benefits for students too. This chapter will address some basic as well as advance users' tips for using Google classroom for students.

3.1 Accepting an Invitation & Joining a Class

To accept an invitation from your teacher

- Go to classroom.google.com.
- In the class stream, click Join.

If your teacher included a class overview, click about it at the top.

To join a class

In order to receive assignments from your teacher, manage the work, and communicate with your classmates, you must first sign in to the classroom and join the class of your teacher.

You have two ways to join a class:

- If you're given a class code by your instructor, use that code to add yourself to the class.
- If your professor is sending an invitation, open the course stream, and click on the class card to join.

3.2 Viewing Work on the Work Page

When using a computer to access Google classroom

To show research on Google Classroom set by the teacher.

The upcoming and unfinished job is on the chapter card, due within a week.

- Go to the google.com.

If there's upcoming work for each class, you'll see the title and the due date.

- (Optional) Click a title to see any instructions.

To view work within the class stream

- Go to classroom.google.com.
- Click the class.
- Click a title to see any instructions or feedback.
- (Optional) Click on Add class comment or number class comment at the top to add a class comment. Type in your comment and press Mail. (Everyone in the class will access this)
- (Optional) Click on Add a private comment to submit a private message to your instructor. Type in your comment and click Mail. (This can be read-only by the teacher)

To view work on the work page

- Go to classroom.google.com.
- Click Menu Work.
- Click a title.
- (Optional) To add a comment to the class, click on Add comment to class. Type in your comment and click Mail. (For all class views)
- (Optional) Click Add a private comment to send a private message to your instructor. Type in your comment and click Mail. (For a teacher to comment only)
- (Optional) Go back to the Job tab to filter your job by class. Click all classes, and choose a class.
- (Optional) To show any work you have already submitted, please click at the top. Tap on a heading to see some feedback.

When using an Android or IPad to access Google classroom

To view work within the class stream

- Tap the Classroom.

- Tap the class name.
- Tap a title to see any instructions.
- Tap Your Work to see your work.

To View work on the work page

- Tap the Classroom.
- At the top, tap Menu.
- Tap Work.
- Tap a title to see any instructions or feedback.
- (Optional) To see work you already submitted, go back to the Work page, and the tap was done. Open the work to see any feedback.

To view work in the class stream

- Tap the Classroom.
- Tap the class name.
- Tap a title to see any instructions.
- Tap Your Work to see your work.

To view work on the work page

- Tap the Classroom.
- At the top, tap Menu.
- Tap Work.
- Tap the title to see any feedback or instructions.
- (Optional) Go back to the Work page to see the work you've already submitted, and the tap is done. Open to see any feedback about the work.

3.3 How Students Complete and Submit Assignments?

Turn in − if something has to be applied to the project, follow the steps to turn the job into.

Mark done − if you do not add any connection to the task, follow the steps to mark a completed task.

After you apply it, you can edit an assignment. Any assignment which is turned in or marked after the due date is considered late, however.

Using a computer

Your teacher can view and edit files that you add or build for a task before you press Switch In. This can be beneficial if you need to check a file with your instructor before you formally submit an assignment.

In Google Docs, if you have the assignment open, simply click Turn in at the top corner.

If necessary, you will have the option to add a private message to your teacher too.

- Go to the.google.com.
- Press on the name, then click on the assignment.

Note: On the Job Page or in the Class Calendar, you can also access the assignments.

- If your teacher is using Google Forms, press the form below, and answer your question. Press Switch In.

If the form is the only work done, it simply marks your task.

- Click Open Task when there is some work to be done on the assignment.
- Click the thumbnail to open and check if your teacher has attached a Google Drive item.

(Optional) To attach an item

- Click the arrow Down next to Connect.
- Click the Link, Drive, or File button.
- Select the attachment or insert it and click Add.

(Optional) To create a new attachment

Press the Down arrow next to Build, and choose the type of file. A new file will appear for you, your job.

- Click on the file and enter your info.
- (Optional) Click on Remove to remove an attachment.
- (Optional) To add a private message, type it in the box, and press Send.

Click Turn in and confirm.

Modifications to assignment status are made.

To mark an assignment done

- Go to the.google.com.
- Click on section, then click on the task.

Note: Your assignments can also be accessed on the Work page or in the class calendar.

- (Optional) Fill in your teacher's private comment if necessary.
- Press and check on the Label as made.

Edit your assignment after turning in or marking done

After turning in or marking done edit your assignment

- Go to the.google.com.
- Click on a name then clicks on the task.
- Click Confirm and Unsubmit.

Important: Your status changes to Unsubmitted for this assignment, so be sure to resubmit it before the due date.

- Make alterations.
- (Optional) Add any new or connected data.
- (Optional) Fill in your teacher's private message.
- Press Turn In and confirm.

The status of the assignment changes to do

Important: Any assignment that's turned in or marked done after the due date is marked late.

Submit an assignment

How you submit an assignment depends on whether or not you have anything to attach.

There are two options:

Turn in — if anything has to be added to the task, follow the steps to turn the task into.

Mark did — if you do not add any addition to the task, follow the steps to mark a completed assignment.

After you apply it, you can edit an assignment. Any assignment which is turned in or labeled after the due date is considered late, however.

When using an android device.

Your teacher can display and edit files that you add or create for an assignment before you press Turn In. It can be helpful if you need to review a file with your professor before you officially apply an assignment.

- Classroom Tap.
- Tap on the label.

Note: You can also view your assignments on the Class Calendar or Worklist.

- Press on the allocation.
- Tap the thumbnail to open and check if your teacher has attached an object.
- Click Your Job.
- (Optional) To add an element to it: Tap Add attachment.
- Tap Drive, File, Link. Take a picture or take a video.
- Pick the attachment or enter it, and tap Select.
- (Optional) To build a new annex: Tap Add annex.

- Click New Documents, New Images, New Sheets, or New PDF files.
- Enter your details and tap finished once you created a new text, presentation, or spreadsheet.
- Once you've created a new PDF, it opens as a blank file, and you can write notes or draw pictures. When done, click Save.
- (Optional) Tap Delete, and confirm, to delete an attachment.
- (Optional) To add your teacher's private message, type it in the box, and tap Post.
- Tap Turn In and confirm.
- Changes to assignment status are completed.

Mark an assignment is done

- Classroom Press.
- Tap on that class.

We can also access your assignments on the Class Calendar or Job page.

- Tap the assignment, then click Your Work.
- Tap and confirm with a mark as done.

Edit your assignment after turning in or marking done

- Tap Classroom.
- Tap the class.
- Tap the assignment and then tap Your Work.
- Tap Un-submit and confirm.

Note: Your status for this assignment changes to Unsubmitted so make sure you resubmit it before the due date.

- Make any changes.
- (Optional) Attach any new files or links.
- (Optional) Add a private note to your teacher and tap Post.

- Tap Resubmit and confirm.

The status of the assignment changes to done.

Important: Any assignment made after the due date that is turned in or marked is late marked.

Submit an assignment

How you submit an assignment depends on whether or not you have anything to attach.

There are two options:

Turn in — if anything has to be added to the task, follow the steps to turn the task into.

Mark did — if you do not add any connection to the task, follow the steps to mark a completed assignment.

After you submit it, you can edit an assignment. Any assignment which is turned in or marked after the due date is considered late, however.

You can view and edit the instructor before you press Turn-In when using an IPad Files that you add to or build for an assignment. This can be beneficial if you need to check a file with your instructor before you formally submit an assignment.

- Classroom Press.
- Tap on that class.

Note: The tasks can also be found on the Job page or in the class calendar.

- Tap on the number.
- Tap the thumbnail to open and check if your teacher has attached an object.

(Optional) To attach an item:

- Press Attachment to Add.
- Tap Drive, Link, Choose a picture, or use a camera.

- Tap the selected file or press Add.
- (Optional) To create a new annex: Tap Add annex.
- Click New Documents, New Images, New Sheets, or New PDF files.
- Insert your details and tap finished when you created a new text, presentation, or spreadsheet.
- When you've created a new PDF, it opens as a blank file, and you can write notes or draw pictures. After done, tap Save.
- (Optional) Tap Remove and confirm to remove an attachment.
- (Optional) Enter it in the box and tap Post to add a private message to your instructor.

- Tap Switch In and confirm.
- Modifications to assignment status are made.

When you have finished an assignment

Tap the Classroom.

- Tap the class.
- Tap the assignment.
- Tap Mark as done and confirm.

The status of the assignment changes is done.

To edit your assignment after turning in or marking done

- Tap Classroom.
- Tap the class.
- Tap the assignment.
- Tap Unsubmit and confirm.

Remember, your status changes to Unsubmitted for this assignment, so make sure you resubmit it before the due date.

- Make any necessary changes.
- (Optional) Attach any new files or links.

- (Optional) To add a private comment to your teacher, enter it in the box and tap Post.
- Tap Turn In and confirm.

How Students Complete & Submit Assignments

Students can view active assignments by clicking on a specific class they are part of and reviewing the upcoming assignments when they login to Google Classroom. A more efficient way, however, is to press the menu button in the upper left corner of the screen and pick Assignments from the pop-out display. It shows students a list of assignments for all of their classes, as well as those in which they turned in, which ones are still pending and which ones are overdue. Assignments that the teacher has graded will also be shown with a grade next to them here.

Clicking on one of those assignments will open the student's related paper. If it is a Google Drive file, in the top right hand corner, next to the Share button, an additional button is added to the toolbar. This button has the "Turn it in" mark. Clicking on it submits to the instructor their task.

As of now, there's no way to "turn in" YouTube videos or URLs that the teacher has assigned to students, but that probably will change too soon.

Students are able to view all the assignments they have assigned via the sidebar menu.

3.4 Google Classroom- Advanced User Tips for Students

Did your teacher send you an invitation to join a class at Google Classroom recently? The chances are you may not have heard about the software before now that most of the schools and colleges are closed, teachers use this Google offer to create virtual classes and share assignments.

Meanwhile, students can directly upload their work online, show their assignment scores, review class reviews, and even engage with other students or teachers using Google Classroom in a healthy discussion.

It's the perfect time to get to know what Google is offering. The best part about it is able to use it both on the web and on mobile platforms. Tutors should test our teacher's guide on the tips and tricks on Google Classroom.

In this post, we'll mention ten of the best tips and tricks for students on Google Classroom. We recommend integrating them into your routine and efficiently accomplishing assignment submissions.

Customize your google drive folder

When dealing with 5 to 6 classes at a time in Google Classroom, customizing them in Google Drive is always advisable, so that you don't end up mixing the assignments. As you might know, in a specific Google Drive folder, your teacher would arrange all the required documents and material resources.

Google driver color

You can go to Google Drive Class > Classwork, and open the new tab folder. Right-click on it and change the color of the folder, or rename it. That's one of the smart ways to keep your folders separate from your personal projects and separate your schoolwork.

Add class comment on an assignment

Google Classroom allows you to comment on a class assignment. Except for the one around the assigned task, you may not wish to engage in the general discussion.

You can go to Community > Classwork > select any assignment > See assignment and add a comment. The comment will be clear to the whole class.

Use google apps to submit work

As already mentioned, Google Classroom also integrates other Google apps and services. You can submit your assignments using YouTube Video, Google Docs file, Google Sheets file, or even Google Drawing file.

Send work Open Class > Classroom > Open an assignment and tap add or create under the menu. It will open a sliding menu where you can add files from different sources-Google Drive, direct link, attach a file, and even create new documents.

Unsubmit work

In certain cases, that is useful. Say you mistakenly sent the wrong file for an assignment. That can happen as you may be dealing with dozens of files across the classroom and with personal work. Click on the assignment you submit, and the Unsubmit button appears to undo the submission. You know what else to do.

View your work

As a student, you might want to take a periodic look at your work and deadlines. Many times, keeping track of submissions can be confusing. And you may end up missing the project deadline.

View work

You can open a class > Classwork > View Your Work, and here you can see all the work assigned with title, date, attached file, and more. Use the side filter menu also to streamline the list.

Use private comments

We may not want to engage in the general discussion if you have specific doubts or queries as it would be accessible to everyone in the class.

Google Classroom offers the feature of Private Comments to talk directly to the teachers. The discussion remains private to the rest of the class and is not apparent.

Open a class, go to Classwork > view assignment, and you'll see the Private Comments section on the right. Use it to talk privately with teachers about the project. When using Class comments in an assignment, it will be visible to the whole class.

Customize class notifications

Dealing with multiple classes at a time can confuse all incoming notifications with you. Google Classroom is happy to let you customize them.

Tap the hamburger menu from the Google Classroom app and go to Settings. For all the comments and classes, you are enrolled in, you will see the notifications toggles. Adjust them to suit your needs.

Customize notifications

Tap Class Notification to control updates by class, and you can see all of your enrolled classes here. Cast the unnecessary ones off.

Turn off email notifications

Google Classroom also sends out email alerts about the new class updates, in addition, to push notification. For a busy classroom, the practice will easily fill in the Gmail inbox space. Suggest turning off the option Setup.

Turn off email

View grade, private comments submitted by teachers

By now, we bet you know your teachers can use Google Classroom's private comment function as well.

By going into Classwork > View your work, you can view them and check the grades for the submitted work.

Use the filter menu and select the option ' Returned with the grade, 'and the teacher will be able to view grades as well as private comments for submission.

Unenroll the class

Did you get the lesson done? Is the semester over, or has the mission finished? A student can unsubscribe from a Google Classroom class. Tap the three-dot menu from the homepage, and choose an unenrolled class.

Chapter 4: Additional Tips for Effective Use of Google Classroom

Over the past two years, Google Classroom has become a popular learning platform for many teachers as well as students using G Suite for Education. This chapter will highlight the problems related to the use of this platform, as well as their solutions.

4.1 Most Common Issues of Remote Learning and their Solutions

Problems of online training and how to solve them

Game learn Team Human Resources

The education and learning world is on the move towards online training. The advantages are undeniable: reduced costs, better versatility for the student, and the opportunity to potentially train thousands of people across the globe. In addition, you can track what students are doing at any given moment, so it breaks with the boredom so passivity of classroom courses.

E-learning, however, isn't without its shortcomings. Online training comes with its own particular features, which can jeopardize (or limit) the training's performance. Let's not see e-learning as a panacea. It is only by knowing the problems encountered by other companies and institutions that you can implement programs to realize its full potential.

Therefore, we identified the eight major issues of online training in this book. But don't worry, we have come up with a solution for them all.

Problem 1: Online training is boring

Although online training is intended to provide a solution to classroom-based learning boredom, this isn't always the case. Many e-learning courses consist of endless texts accompanied by a long list of multiple-choice questions which do not include students. It just seems like e-reading rather than e-learning.

These types of courses often mean students get bored with online training, and this lack of engagement and motivation is one of the main reasons why e-learning courses fail. Students clearly do not want to take the class, do not have access to the program, and do not complete the course. MOOCs (massive open online courses) are a good example: only 10 % of students who register for a course do actually complete it.

Solution: Find a new, enjoyable, and immersive Online Course Be sure to find an interactive, creative, and enjoyable online course that will prevent the students from getting bored. Although this may have been challenging in the early days of e-learning, it's much simpler nowadays: there are currently a number of providers offering both sorts of interactive training, with challenges and experiences to provide, videos, animation, gamified approaches, practical simulators, and game-based learning.

And there are other ways to offer if you want to add an extra motivating touch to the training. For example, experience has shown that when students receive an official credential or certificate at the end of a course, they become more interested in the training. You can also promote competition by including lists, ratings, and prizes (cash or other rewards) of the winners. All of these will improve employee engagement, and learners are not only more likely to complete the course, but above all, to learn more and more.

Problem 2: Students encounter technical difficulties

Although this may sound obvious, the technological problems are one of the key stumbling blocks in online training. Compatibility issues very often occur (with operating systems, browsers, or smartphones), the courses never get off the ground, or the student doesn't know how to proceed. All of this adds to their frustration, and reduces employee involvement, disrupts the learning experience, and they are likely to give up the course.

Solution: Provide multi-device preparation and personal attention

Keep it simple when facing that challenge. Choose online courses with a strong and clear script that doesn't need much internal memory or high-speed Internet access. Offer priority to courses where no programs need to be downloaded or documents written. Beware of the sound quality (an issue that is often overlooked) when you take the training before your students and be sure to try out the course on several smartphones, browsers, and operating systems.

Problem 3: The students don't know the course exists

This often happens: you've been planning an online course for months, you've selected the best provider, and you know the course is important to your workers. but no one in the company is aware of its existence. Students have hundreds and thousands of courses at their disposal and are often overwhelmed by the workload and everyday routine. As a consequence, nobody knows what the training course is about, and is therefore not taking it.

Solution: Launch a marketing plan

If you want your students to pay real attention to you, consider starting any training plan like a Hollywood movie premiere and using the chain emails to generate excitement or place large posters around the office (for example, along the lines of "Wanted" or "Coming soon"). All this will spark interest from the students, and even before the training begins, you will have created a buzz. Make sure you explain why employee training is necessary and how it can help them become better employees and better people.

At the same time, be sure to communicate the training to your supervisors and to all heads of department. Online classes work much better if you are able to include the company's senior staff based on the experience of different organizations. Not only are senior staff in a position to give their team members time to attend the training, but they may also lead by example and thereby inspire workers to lower down the organization to take the training.

Problem 4: Students don't have time for online training

The e-learning format gives students tremendous flexibility: they can take the courses at their own speed and without any physical constraints, when and where they want. Yet too much versatility also leads to inaction. Time passes, and the student still hasn't reached or completed the training program.

Solution: Set a time limit and give a callback

First of all, to solve this problem, ensure that the courses are divided into several parts and consist of brief lessons, which can be completed in a short time. If students experience big learning stumbling blocks, they'll probably never find the time to tackle them. Divide the courses and conquer them.

Second, don't think about setting a time-limit. The fact that the workout is online does not mean that you cannot set deadlines. Establish a clear and easy timetable showing when any part of the online course should have been completed by the student. Additionally, give notices to students telling them they are out of time and encouraging them to complete the course.

Problem 5: Students need to talk to people

Online courses have many benefits, but we must also recognize their limitations. Students may sometimes get frustrated because of a lack of human contact, a teacher's absence, and an inability to discuss it with their classmates. Often, the online environment may become too small for the student, no matter how enriching it may be, and they will need a physical space where they can solve their queries and practice using real resources.

Solution: Personal attention, social media, and fora

If this is the problem, then one solution is to encourage as much as possible personal interaction within the online world. You can arrange webinars, group work, or forums where students can answer their questions and solve them. It is important that students have an instructor who they can contact (e.g., tutoring via Skype). You may also be encouraging social media use during training, thus providing an additional opportunity for social interaction and humanizing the learning process.

Another solution is to combine online training with some form of classroom training. This form of mixed training (known as blended learning) has been shown to strengthen what the students have learned and increase the educational value of the curriculum.

Therefore, if you have been able to coordinate debates with the instructor before, after, or after the course, between students or classes, this way, you'll combine the online and offline worlds and solve one of e-learning's most noticeable limitations.

Problem 6: Students can't practice

Science has shown that the best way to learn something is to practice it (the popular learning by doing definition). We can only internalize and recall the content and skills we are learning by practicing the things we do and experiencing (experiential learning). Many online courses, however, overlook this part and focus exclusively on theoretical content and external lessons. Students are, therefore, unable to practice, and the learning process is not reaching its full potential.

Solution: Using realistic and useful courses which have simulators

An important prerequisite for students to learn is the quality and practicality of the courses. Employees must feel (though selfishly) that the training will be useful to them in their day-to-day work and will help them to become better professionals (and people, indeed). If e-learning courses fulfill the criteria, students in the real world should be able to put into practice what they know.

Additionally, you can use simulators to ensure they get to practice during the online course. Simulators (for example, by pilots and surgeons) have been used for decades to simulate real-life conditions so students can train and experiment in healthy and controlled environments. By integrating simulators into your training course, you will be able to solve this problem and ensure that your students put their new skills and knowledge into practical usage.

Problem 7: The quality of the courses is mediocre

The standard of the courses is medium driven by students, the content of the course sounds interesting, a communication campaign was launched, so everyone knows about it, but the quality of the content is not equal. With today's world's information overload, thousands of free online courses, and powerful platforms like Wikipedia, YouTube, and Google, the content of the course must be excellent and of the highest standard. Nonetheless, many students end up frustrated when they discover that they can learn more on their own than with their companies or institutions offering simple, mediocre courses.

Solution: Offer nothing but the best The world has dramatically changed in the last few years, and so has your job. One of your most important missions as the person responsible for the training is to find, select, and prioritize the best courses. Remember: it's got to be better than Google. So just go for the ultimate.

Problem 8: The online course has no impact on your organization

The online course does not affect your organization. Sometimes, e-learning can solve all of the above problems. The students accessed the training platform, no technical problems were encountered, and they completed the course within the deadline and were able to practice what they had learned. Has that improved the human capital of your business? Do you have results that you can present to your superiors? Many e-learning projects fail because they have not had an overall impact on the organization.

Solution: Align online courses with the goals of your organization (and measure them!) The best way to solve this problem is to plan ahead of training start.

You need to be explicit about your learning objectives, and why you want your students to take this online course. Most importantly, the training is aligned with the interests of your firm or institution. Hence, you should choose materials that will actually contribute to the overall goals of the organization (such as increased company sales, increased employee awareness of a particular issue, or improved customer service management).

What's more, ensure that the training outcomes are calculated. Set indicators, and measure them again after completion of the course, before implementing the project. You will thus know what impact the training had on your organization.

4.2 Tips for Motivating and Engaging Students for Remote/e-Learning

Strategies for Engaging e-learning students

You might have been asking, "How can I make my students more active in online discussions or in class discussions?" or "How can I make them more interested in what they learn and do?"

Engaging e-learning students and taking part in events

You could have noticed a decline in student engagement and learning with the introduction of eLearning and hybrid courses. One should recognize various forms of interactivity when developing or teaching online or blended courses, such as learner engagement with content, teachers, and peers. Course design is a crucial element in the determination of interactivity efficiency, quantity, and type1.

Trigger awareness prior to use

The incentive of students to learn will be improved if new learning is related to their previous experience.

When learners' existing knowledge is enabled, and with new learning, they see the importance of it, they can organize and understand the new information more easily; therefore, they will be more interested in their learning process.

Ask them what their goals are?

Understanding what the expectations of the students are in a course is very helpful in the creation and delivery of the course materials. This can also help to personalize the learning of the students as they feel a sense of control over their learning. It can also help create connections between teacher and student, as they will feel the encouragement you offer them by asking them about their objectives. Knowing what its aims are will help you build more meaningful and real-life examples that are useful in enhancing your learning.

Have their goals in mind when teaching

When designing or creating materials and teaching in class, always keep in mind the goals of the students, knowing what the aspirations of the students are would allow you to have strategic scaffolds when necessary; thus, they feel the progress they make in their learning. They'll be more involved and motivated when the students know they 're learning.

Figure out what their desires are and have them motivated to want more

You may have taught students who were pressured to do a specific course by their parents or promoters without their participation in that course. It is a teacher's greatest challenge as he/she has to teach students who hate the course and are completely disoriented in class.

They send you the body language and the signal that I am not interested in what you say or do in class. We still come up with reasons for not taking part in class / online discussions or getting their assignments completed.

You've had these students, I 'm sure, and you've either decided to give up on them or get them interested. Ask them what it's like to do in their free time, or actually enjoy it. You may then also create your class assignments or discussion topics in order to fit them in. For example, if they enjoy watching films, you might ask them to watch a film that you suggest, discuss characters, critique or summarize the theme. It depends, of course, on the subject you are teaching, and what objectives you are learning. This will help to increase their curiosity in having more because you have expressed your desire to them.

Ask them to share their challenges with you and class

Instructors will also be mindful of what their students are feeling, with the diversity of learners in mind. Others are slow learners, and some are fast learners. When learners find it hard to understand those concepts, or do a particular assignment based on your expectations, encourage them to openly share it with you or class. Since some students are more introverted and may not find it easy to share it with their peers in class, you may ask them to use twitter or blogs set for this reason. Those reserved may find it easier to write, rather than to speak. This will also improve the relationship between students and their classmates, and they will realize the value of group learning and support from each other that they can get. Often some learners may feel like they are the only ones with difficulties, believing that the majority of the class is straightforward about everything that is taught or assigned. When they share this online, they know that they're not alone in their path of learning. And it is you, as the professor, who should offer trust in your classroom setting.

Connect and interact with them

When you follow the above tips, they will help you to communicate.

Yet let them feel your presence and encouragement by thanking them for their efforts, even if they are not there yet, even when they are desperate to reach you. Often demonstrate your participation in online discussions by commenting on some posts or debating some positive posts in class.

Show them how to learn

Since online learning for some students is very recent, they may not be fully conscious of the change to be made in their study habits. For others, whether you are creating online lessons for adult learners or teaching adult learners, it may be the first time you take an online course. They should be asked whether they are learning well by having them reflect on their progress in learning. You should also express why you are asking them to do those tasks, like a discussion board. The justification for their learning needs to be transparent to adult learners, as this increases their motivation when they see the importance of what they are charged with doing and what they plan to do after completing a course.

Use real-life scenarios

For the adult learners will know what they are doing. If they see the importance of what they are studying in real life, they will be more engaged. You can build case studies or real-life scenarios in any context which drive the motivation and interest of learners to know more.

Build a sense of community

One online learning challenge is that students often feel pretty isolated. Consider how you can make direct contact with as many learners as possible through emails, instant messages, and video, helping them see how you're investing in their learning.

In addition, promote opportunities for learners to see each other as partners through approaches, including peer interaction and peer review, as well as potentially helping students find peers to research with.

Help students feel like they can succeed

When learners believe they will excel, they are more likely to continue. Consider how to organize tasks so that on the way to more demanding challenges students will encounter "fast wins" Furthermore, seeing how similar peers have advanced will help inspire a student who would otherwise feel unlikely to succeed; See if more online learning experienced students are willing to share some of their ideas on how to excel in the course.

Establish ways to monitor progress

If students are not sure how they're doing, they may not engage in productive engagement. Establish and communicate explicit goals for the course as well as tie student activities back to those goals and progress. Look for tools in your online program (e.g., practice instant feedback questions, study organizers checking off when students use various services, etc.) that can help students stay on top of their progress. Be clear on how you think these resources will help students use them to see the potential value in them, and suggest them.

Reward and celebrate success

While it is true that learning is a reward of its own, everybody can now and then use some help to stick to their objectives. Talk of ways to offer incentives to students, whether they're in the form of encouragement, point to their grades, or any common objective the class works towards. Focus on rewarding good effort, progress, and the kinds of learning behaviors you want to see more than just accomplishment.

Relate class to students' lives

It can be difficult to be motivated when we do not see the meaning of what we do. The relation to our daily lives is one significant source of interest for academic learning. How can I use what I am in classroom learning to advance my career, achieve my goals, or support my friends, family and community? Give some possible links like these to students and also encourage them to try to make those links themselves!

4.3 Effective Strategies for Using Google Classroom

Strengthen your efficiency by following classroom strategies written below:

Google Classroom Techniques to Use Now

First of all, The Big One.

Hide and save (don't delete) packaged and posted assignments you haven't accessed during class time.

Google Classroom currently doesn't require teachers to cover assignments that have already been uploaded. This really makes some sense when you think about all the ways a single assignment posted in the classroom embeds itself through Google Drive and Calendar on the side about stuff Google does.

But for teachers, that can be a painful problem. Pick the situation up.

Let's say that the night before my English class, I posted a stunning short story practice. The text is attached in the form of of.pdf. It also includes two hand-picked video clips, as is a collaborative reflection activity attached as a Google Doc. In Google Slides, a supplementary tool introduces the students to specific literary tools.

And I posted a specified learning target and incorporated instructions in the summary of the assignment.

That took at least five minutes — maybe more — to bring all of those tools together and post them as an assigned task.

But instead, the day occurs, and we don't get to the thing that is being prepared. There's something else that gets in the way, and we never get a chance to get into it.

I have a tough decision left to me.

Should I delete the post before our next meeting, and build it again? Or do I leave the post up, just change the due date and embrace the fact that some students will read the plot, watch the photos, explore the Google Slides, and essentially absorb the entire activity before the next class?

There is a workaround to this issue.

Everything I did was create a Classroom dummy called Staging Area. Whenever I'm in a situation like the one I've described, I use the Re-Post command to copy the entire assignment into my Classroom Staging Area. Then I remove it from the actual classroom in which it will inevitably remain.

So none of my plans are lost, and I don't repeat the entire post-cycle the next day. My wonderful short story work is saved — no spoilers. I simply re-post the Staging Area assignment back into the right classroom before the next lesson, and we're back on track.

Enable real-time feedback for presentations

Do a major favor to yourself and your learners by copying and pasting test models into any private statement prior to presentations.

Include spaces for an overall evaluation, success criteria, and emoji stars and wishes, etc. with spaces for each student in your class to get feedback.

With all this put in place before student presentations, I can provide real-time, accurate, and informative feedback to students — whilst they are present. It means I don't assess their presentations after school, and they don't wait for feedback.

Below is the test summary that I pasted before their last Genius Hour presentations into all the private feedback of my students.

Use emoji's to code learning activities

Begin each unit title and assign a name with an emoji theme,

And send completed units and assignments an emoji checkmark to indicate in a glance they are behind us.

Include learning targets in every posted activity or assignment

That's not as much a convenience event as it's great pedagogy.

It will often send you back to the unit plan or the standard curricular, keeping you grounded. And reminding the students what the goal of each learning activity is will always be present.

"Why should we do this?"

Get a quick sense of your students' progress

I often post self-assessments in Google Classroom, especially in Units of Math. They are a simple but powerful way for me to gather data on the learning and progress of my students, which will inform my next moves.

I get those results by asking a multiple-choice question right in the classroom. Tap on any bar, and I see which students have chosen the skill level.

Pass homeroom Classrooms with all teachers who teach the same degree as you do

This makes it easy and quick for teachers to keep tabs on where their peers are in the curriculum and see what they've been doing recently, and it's also an easy way to share resources. If I drop into Chelsea's Classroom, I can use the Re-Post command to drop it straight into my classroom, and I like how she has set up a learning activity.

Share homeroom Classes with all specialist staff

Let your language teachers, art teachers, and band teachers remove announcements and tools from your classroom. But if they don't, a great alternative is having access to your classroom.

Post once to multiple Classrooms

Take advantage of the feature if you are a professional instructor. You don't have to post different assignments in every classroom. All relevant Classrooms are posted at once.

Adjust Google Classroom notifications to silence Classroom emails and notifications, which are not yours.

This strategy becomes relevant after discussing the two previous strategies about discussing Google Classrooms. Switch off Classroom Notifications you don't teach.

If you do not take this step, alerts from any resubmission of assignments or from any private comments made by any student in any classroom will be received by email. Some teachers and EAs at my building have access to up to 10 or even more Classrooms. That makes for a lot of notifications!

You can counter this by limiting notifications to only the classrooms you teach. With that said, respond to private comments where possible. There'll be some very good communication there for some students.

Structure weekly times to review email inboxes and organize classroom assignments for your homeroom students.

Email is boring for most middle- and high-schoolers. My stepson is 8th grade would tell us. They do not care.

Yet the classroom encourages useful e-mail communication between teachers and students. I can post feedback in private classroom comments showing up in the form of an email for the students. I could even email selected students to remind them to submit an assignment, post announcements of an upcoming event, or post-self-assessment check-in to monitor learning. Most of all, these communications run on email, so students should check their inbox once a week.

They are not going to do it on their own, and we can't expect them to. Each week we have to set aside 15 minutes or more to ensure this life ability is happening.

Some would say email is not going to be around forever, and maybe they are right. But for the last 25 years, it has been working well, and it will not be going anywhere anytime soon. Ensure sure the students are learning how to maximize the inbox.

Create a school-wide Google Classroom

This allows for school-wide polls, debates, hot lunch order form submissions, yearbook photo submissions for the student, announcements delivery, etc.

Full disclosure: I am not currently using this — partly in an attempt to slow down the flow of ideas I'm pushing on colleagues in a new teaching community. But at a previous school, I set up this, and it works wonders.

For administrators: create a Google Classroom for staff teachers, with teachers as teachers, and teachers as students.

This is a perfect way for email traffic to be minimized. Conduct fast and effective surveys of workers. Post "assignments" such as plans for professional growth, and allow "students" (teachers) to submit when completed. Or post reporting tools and open commentaries so that teachers can view posts as boards of discussion.

Smarter Ways to Classroom Google

Google Classroom is slowly becoming the most effective technical platform in education.

It may lack the visual appeal of the iPads or the student credibility of a BYOD program. It may not be as forward-thinking as we would like here at Teach Thought, but Google Classroom excels in providing solutions for a wide range of teachers with a variety of expertise and comfort level with the education technology. It also makes use of the familiar Google template that many teachers have used for years. For many teachers right here right now, in many classrooms, it scratches the itch.

So, underneath are at least things you can do with Google Classroom. As new ideas come in, the platform changes and we learn more on our own about its subtleties, we'll update this list.

Smarter Ways to Google Classroom:

- If an assignment, lesson, or unit doesn't work, add your own comments – or have students add their own feedback), tag it, or save it to another revision folder.
- Align resume with other teachers.
- To share data with a community of professional learners.
- Do you keep specimens written for planning?
- Tag your résumé.
- Use Google Forms to request daily, weekly, by-semester, or annual feedback from students and parents.
- Exchange anonymous excerpts of writing with students;

- From the point of view of the students, see what your assignments look like.
- Flip the classroom open. Google Apps for Education has, at its core, the tools for publishing videos and sharing assignments.
- Communicate with students about assignment criteria.
- Let the students ask in private questions.
- Let the students create their own digital work portfolios.
- Create a list of approved sources of information. You can also distinguish this by the student, group, level of reading, and more.
- Post a student or student and parent advertising.
- Create more virtual learning opportunities for your students – for example, in the higher end.
- Use Google Sheets to map the students' own development over time.
- Share the due dates with mentors in a public calendar outside the classroom.
- Students email individually, or as groups. Better still, watch how they communicate with each other.
- Using Google Forms to create a test that grades itself.
- Command file rights (view, delete, copy, download) on a file-by-file basis.
- Have students curate learning artifacts based on a study.
- As an instructor, you should work with other teachers (same level by the team, the same level of content).
- Encourage digital citizenship through documented peer-to-peer interaction.
- Use Google Calendar for scheduled dates, events outside the classroom, and other relevant "chronological data."
- Interact with students online who can refuse to 'speak' to you in person.
- Cross-curricular workshops streamline with other teachers.

- Assemble and publish commonly accessed websites to ensure that they all have the same access, the same documents, the same links, and the same information.
- Students who are vertically aligned learn by curating and exchanging 'landmark' student assignments that demonstrate mastery of common standards.
- Promote a shared vocabulary and share district-wide expectations by unpacking.
- Enable students to use their smartphones for structured learning. By accessing documents, YouTube channels, community correspondence, digital portfolio components, and more on a BYOD system, students will have the ability to use their phone as something other than a sole entertainment app.
- Develop and publish 'power principles' for accountability and cooperation (with pupils, other teachers, and others).
- Encourage peer-to-peer and/or school-to-school relationships between students and other students, students, and teachers with other teachers.
- For example, create 'by-need' groups as classes – based on the level of reading.
- Check which assignments have students accessed?
- Giving suggestions to graduates.
- Add student-written voice comments (this requires a third-party app to do so).
- Help the students create YouTube channels related to the content.
- 'Closed-circuit publishing' of annotated research papers by different types (MLA, APA, etc.) or otherwise 'confusing' work.
- Share introductions.
- Build a digital car park "for questions.
- Offer digital slips for the exit.

- Delegate volunteer lesson extensions for pupils instead of homework. Look to who has accessed and accomplished what, and when questions arise about mastery or grades.
- Create Miscellaneous lesson material folders. Digital Text Versions, etc.
- Enjoy smarter, easy-to-use conferencing with students and parents, info, writing, reviews, data access, etc.
- Save pdf or other digital resource snapshots into universally accessed folders.
- Build a data wall along with color coding and spreadsheets.
- Make it easy to access sub-work or makeup work.
- Gather data 4. This can happen in a variety of ways, from using Google Forms, Google Sheets extraction, or your own in-house method.
- Give the learning prompt feedback.
- Fifty-seven. See who got what – and when – at-a-glance completed.
- Track the students turning in to work.
- When access is tracked, look for patterns in student habits–those who instantly access assignments, those who regularly return to work, and so on–and convey those trends (anonymously) to students when a way of communicating 'best practices in learning' to students who might not otherwise know.
- Differentiate instruction by tiering, grouping, or spiraling Bloom.
- Build classes based on preparation, interest, level of reading, or other educational and learning factors;
- Use Google Forms for student polling, create reader interest surveys, and more.
- Cite page Model works.
- Build datasheets.
- Digital team-building design activities;
- Build a classroom that is paperless.

- Share common and regularly accessed assignments – project instructions, year-long due dates, math formulas, information about the subject field, historical timelines, etc.

Conclusion

A very good alternative to the more conventional management packages (ex. Microsoft Office) is the Google class room. Not only does Google class room alter the nature of teacher-student interaction, but it can also alter the way students communicate. The advantages of cloud computing are various. Google Classroom is a front-end interface for G Suite for Education, actually. It's a platform that encourages teachers to transfer to the internet some of their typical classroom work, rather than moving their entire program into an online world. This may be enough for many educators, particularly those employed at schools who are wary of (or maybe unable to support) technological adventurism. Google Classroom lowers the technological, cultural, and institutional barriers for those educators to experiment with online education. I find Google Classroom to make it easy for students to interact and to educate them about what's right. This book has lots of genuinely useful features for teachers and students, which could potentially help cut down on paper used in classrooms. Google Classroom is a good basic method. Teachers in schools that don't have a common learning site, it seems ideal. This book will teach you all aspect about google class room that are related to students and teacher and also administration. This book made you job easier and you can learn almost everything just by reading it carefully. To me, those benefits undoubtedly overshadow all potential barriers. I wish you best of luck for your learning journey.

Made in the USA
Coppell, TX
02 December 2020